THE COUNTRY CUPBOARD

KITCHENS

THE COUNTRY CUPBOARD

KITCHENS

IMAGINATIVE TIPS & SENSIBLE ADVICE
FOR DECORATING, EQUIPPING & ENJOYING

PAT ROSS

Watercolors by Carolyn Bucha

FRIEDMAN/FAIRFAX
PUBLISHERS

Contents

A FRIEDMAN/FAIRFAX BOOK

Library of Congress Cataloging-in-Publication data available upon request.

ISBN 1-56799-688-4

Editor: Sharyn Rosart
Art Director: Jeff Batzli
Designer: Devorah Wolf
Production Director: Karen Matsu Greenberg

Color separations by Colourscan Overseas Co Pte Ltd
Printed in Hong Kong by Midas Printing Ltd

1 3 5 7 9 10 8 6 4 2

For bulk purchases and special sales, please contact:
Friedman/Fairfax Publishers
Attention: Sales Department
15 West 26th Street
New York, New York 10010
212/685-6610   FAX 212/685-1307

Visit our website:
http://www.metrobooks.com

Introduction

In search of a user-friendly kitchen, I once took a mental sledgehammer to the wall that separated our kitchen from the dining room and decided it had to go. This was some years ago, when, as new apartment owners, we could finally change more than the paint color. New York City's pre-war apartments are built like forts, so it took burly workmen with sledgehammers days to demolish the wall that separated our formal dining room from a utilitarian kitchen. We wanted our new kitchen to reflect the casual way we lived and cooked; we wanted it to have personality. Our family called the new space the keeping room, and it did indeed keep a range of things over the years, including a big TV, a comfortable sofa, a jammed bookcase, a puppy gate, and two puppies. The room faced a gloomy courtyard; however, in the late afternoon, the sun's glimmering reflections bounced off the windowpanes of the apartment building across the way and filled the kitchen with light, transforming it from a hopelessly stuffy room to a cozy place to share good cooking and good feelings. By opening up the kitchen to the rest of the house, we opened up the heart of our home to family and friends.

Our kitchen styles are as different as we are. From the clean and spare to the fussy and cluttered, we personalize our kitchens to feel comfortable, bring back childhood memories, and so that the kitchen will serve our cooking needs, express our decorating style, and, most significantly, provide a cheerful place to gather. How many times have we thrown a party in a spacious living room or on a breezy porch and found most of the guests having a grand time in the kitchen? Sometimes the kitchen seems more a meeting place than anything else. Perhaps it's the pure symbolism of things kitcheny—of food and nurturing, of nature and its bounty—and the snug way it makes us feel. Moreover, today's kitchen is no longer for women only. Men and kids are partners in both the pleasure and the mess.

There is a sensuous and giving nature to this room. The smells hint of exotic spices and delicious feasts. Our cupboards are treasure troves of variety: peanut butter for filling sandwiches, chicken soup for colds, special teas for cold winter days, an expensive chutney put aside for a special occasion. We tie

bright bows on our homemade herb vinegars and write "Rosemary–for remembrance" on the label. Our offerings are as simple as an apple in a basket or as complicated as a Louisiana gumbo. I've provided both to my kitchen visitors and recall their equal pleasure. Happily, there are no hard and fast rules about kitchens, just a lot of promises about what our kitchens can become.

I'm a good cook of the self-taught variety, with credit going to my mother for the basic, common-sense techniques she passed on to me in our cheerful Maryland kitchen. The honey-pine cabinets with their curlicue edging were made by my father in his basement shop. Surrounding the breakfast nook, the walls were decorated with pretty botanical china plates hung in a neat line. The curtains were trimmed in the ever-so-popular ball fringe of the day that bounced in the breeze like the skirts of a Spanish dancer. As a cosmopolitan New York single woman, I rebelled briefly and carried out a dramatic black-and-white motif in my first kitchen with mixed results. As a newlywed in the 1960s, I remember transforming our ugly refrigerator into a giant checkerboard cube with the ubiquitous Contact paper. Over the years, I've pasted untold yards of wallpaper on kitchen walls, cut hundreds of rolls of shelf paper to fit neatly, searched unsuccessfully for the perfect garlic press, and mastered the melon baller. Needless to say, I've collected great tips, advice, and good old-fashioned know-how from other cooks and other kitchens. Yet it seems there's always something I don't know, or wish I could just remember.

That's why I put together *Kitchens*–to gather together all sorts of useful information in one place.

It's always given me great pleasure to be able to change the look of my kitchen from season to season and year to year without having to call my banker for a loan or hire a carpenter to replace the cabinets. That's why this book opens with "How to Get That Country Look"–ideas for making

easy and effective changes. You can find tips for dressing up your shelves, the best herbs for wreath-making, and ideas for special gifts that come from the kitchen.

I wish I'd had the list of basic cookware and utensils to use when I really needed it or "A Shopping List for a Well-Stocked Pantry" when I moved and my pantry was bare. For those times when you want to create a quick and easy dish without a cook-book, there's a handy chart providing herb seasoning references in addition to a list of herbs for popular ethnic cuisines. The array of vinegars and oils on our store shelves today can be dizzying, so I've included basic descriptions. I could go on, but suffice it to say that this book is meant to be a best friend in the kitchen, offering a bounty of ways to enjoy the heart of your home.

The new apartment I've recently moved in to has a compact, modernist kitchen, but one that opens well beyond into an airy loft-like space for gracious and relaxed living. I can whip up a perfect white sauce and, at the same time, not feel left out of a gathering of friends in the living room. After dinner, the dish-washer sometimes chugs loudly into the rinse cycle and a few missed dessert dishes still sit on the table, but nobody seems to mind. And I wouldn't have it any other way.

–Pat Ross

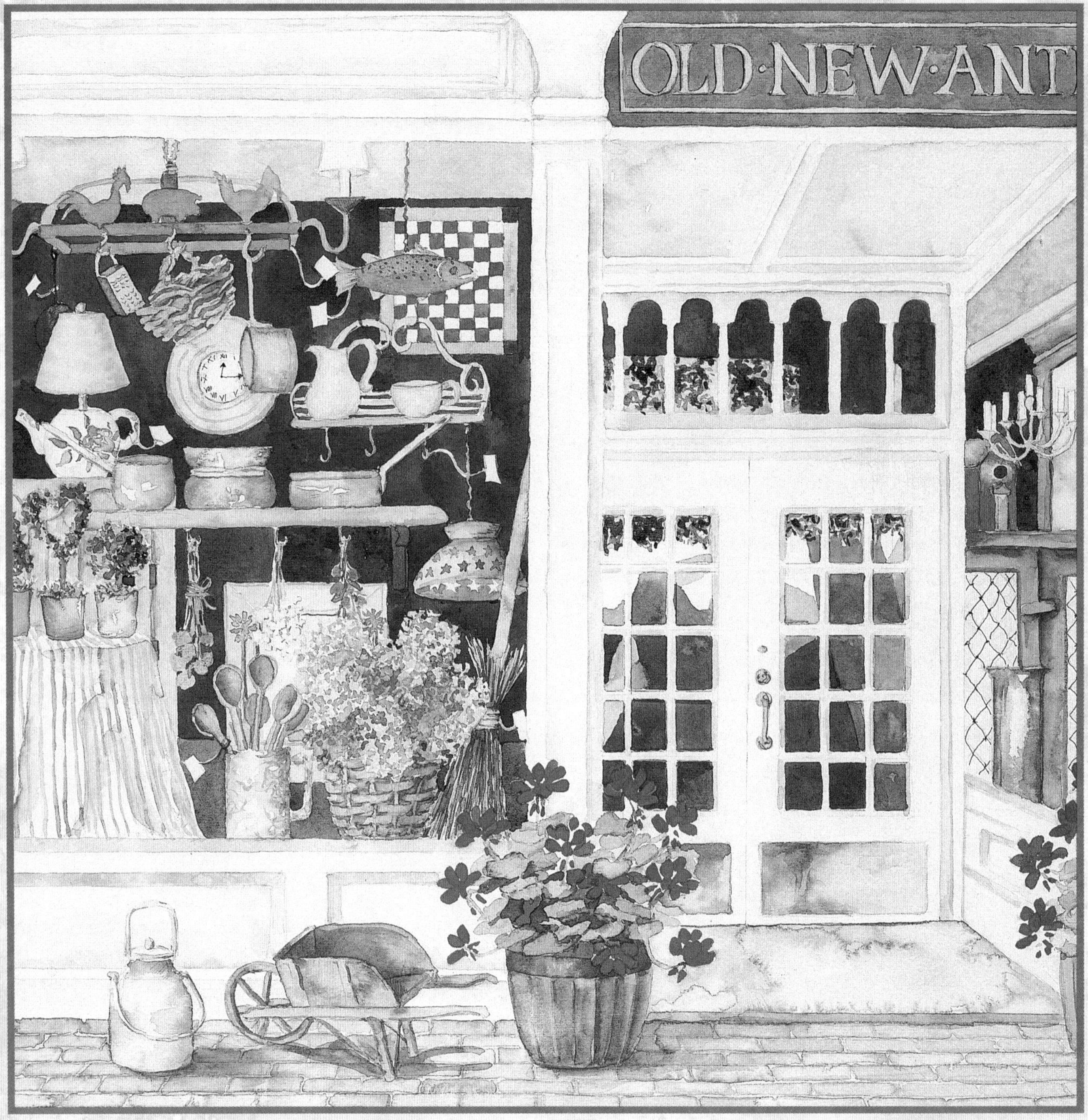
OLD·NEW·ANT

chapter one

Decorating Details for Every Kitchen

HOW TO GET THAT COUNTRY LOOK

Like a quick-change artist, you can make simple and effective decorating changes to transform your kitchen's mood without resorting to expensive renovation and redecoration. By adding a few warm and inviting details, you can bring a fresh look to the kitchen quickly and easily. All you need are a few creative ideas to begin, and the rest will simply unfold.

The first step is choosing a favorite country look–perhaps from one of the three popular looks that follow–and deciding on a basic plan that best suits your time, budget, and lifestyle. You can change the color of the room, rearrange the furniture, recover cushions, and acquire accessories as you locate the perfect combinations. The best advice: take your time and enjoy the process! Visit tag sales, antique shows, and kitchen shops - you'll soon develop a keen eye for true finds and arrive home with the perfect accessories to transform your kitchen.

Think "country kitchen" and three countries frequently come to mind: France, England, and America. These looks are warm, welcoming, and filled with characteristic touches. But it's the combination of these touches that establishes the big picture. With that in mind, here are some ideas to acquaint you with the possibilities as your kitchen decorating adventure begins.

French Country

✦ The bright yellow of the sun in the south of France and the vibrant blue of Mediterranean waters–these are the two perfect colors to establish a French country theme in the kitchen. Apply to walls and cabinets; coordinate with fabric and related accessories.

✦ Paint an old kitchen chair bright blue; place a galvanized tin of strawflowers next to the chair. A sweet child's chair will take on a new life when repainted in white and stenciled with a trailing ivy design.

✦ Give a bare wall new life by adding brickwork, reminiscent of hearths in rustic dwellings. There are do-it-yourself brick kits on the market that can help you accomplish this.

✦ Extend a thick wooden pole or dowel across a counter, then hook on a wonderful assortment of baskets. They'll come in handy for serving everything from baguettes to brie.

'Tis an ill cook that cannot lick his own fingers.

William Shakespeare

◆ Plant pots of mums and other seasonal flowering plants in wooden buckets and place several close to the door for a warm welcome.

◆ Add a clever touch with a pleasant ceramic pig who wears a chef's outfit and holds the evening's menu on a small blackboard. Look for this amusing fellow in kitchen specialty stores and catalogs.

◆ Seek out kitchenware made of weathered iron–pot racks and baker's racks are especially homey–to set a country French mood and provide useful storage at the same time.

◆ What would a French kitchen be without garlic? Add strings of garlic to the pot rack or hang it next to the door. A garlic wreath is pretty, useful, and easily made.

◆ There's never enough copper in the French country kitchen. Hang pots and pans and line up plates along a counter.

◆ Place a row of herb topiaries on a bright windowsill. It's joyful to have fresh rosemary in January.

◆ Fill a tin pitcher with wooden spoons and scoops.

✦ Look for unusual French bistro glasses and store them in plain view.

✦ Use pretty cotton tea towels to make café curtains–stripes, florals, or checks all look charming.

✦ Wish you had more open shelving? Consider removing the doors from an old cupboard. Or remove doors and rehinge in an open reverse position with the door fronts showing.

✦ Stack terra cotta or other colorful plates on open shelves for easy access and attractive display.

✦ Keep yellowware bowls filled with fresh pears and apples.

✦ A shiny brass bar cries out for a line-up of fresh tea towels in bright, cheerful provincial patterns.

✦ Freshly laundered tea towels stacked on an island or counter are a welcome sight–and a subtle hint.

✦ Table linens in toiles and checks are de rigueur for this look.

✦ Sheer fabric shirred and hung behind glass cabinet doors establishes a French country tone–so does cotton lace.

✦ Decorative tiles that speak of things French can stand at the back of the counter, ready to serve as trivets under hot pots and plates.

We may live without friends;
we may live without books;
but civilized man cannot live
without cooks.

Owen Meredith (1921)

+ Don't forget table linens–napkins, table-cloths, and placemats–in cheerful patterns. Sunflower yellows and cornflower blues go with practically everything.

+ Place a wine rack in full view (be sure to keep it away from heat).

+ Large pot racks are popular in many regional decors, but especially well suited to French country.

+ An old weathered cabinet can be given a second life with a quick stripping and color wash. Then tack pieces of chicken wire behind the glass doors. Or replace the glass panes entirely using chicken wire, plain or painted.

+ Faux-finish your walls to give them a timeworn feeling. A ragged or sponged design can be accomplished easily by the beginner. This is a case where neatness doesn't count–the irregularity is part of the charm.

+ Vintage kitchen utensils–mortars, pestles, rolling pins, choppers–can still be found for reasonable prices. Hang them in a line along the wall or use them as accents.

+ A country stepback cupboard that looks at least a hundred years old is always a perfect touch! No one need know it was picked up at a flea market and lovingly refinished by you.

+ Cover your young plants with hothouse bells, or *cloches,* for an authentic French garden look in the kitchen.

+ Add a high shelf to display the objects you'll collect for your French country kitchen, such as pretty plates and small copper collectibles. Consider stain-painting the shelf white or soft green.

✦ Plate racks come in many sizes and have a variety of wonderful uses–from strong iron racks that sit on the floor near the table to pine racks that are often large enough to act as room dividers. If you have pretty dinnerware, it's a shame to keep it hidden behind cabinet doors.

English Country

✦ English kitchens cry out for blue-and-white china–for the table as well as hung on the wall. Antique dessert plates, chips and all, can be hung above the door, over the stove, or anywhere that shows them off. Larger pieces, such as dinner plates and platters, make more dramatic statements on the wall. Be certain to hang them with plate hangers and hooks of the appropriate size and strength.

✦ Pine in a well-scrubbed room says English country. Either plain pine or color-washed pine will work, with a show of knots and graining adding to the appeal. A handsome sideboard or just one special pine chair may be all you need.

✦ Botanical prints in simple gold frames are a wonderfully unexpected–and slightly formal–touch in the English country style kitchen.

✦ The clean lines and ageless purity of white ironstone make it a wonderful selection for tableware. Or display individual plates and other pieces on a kitchen wall, in a narrow adjacent hallway, or over a door. If you build a collection of white ironstone, you'll never run out of serving pieces, display pieces, and decorative accessories for the kitchen and dining room alike.

A delicious sauce will cause you to eat an elephant.

Good Manners (1870)

✦ Use romantic cotton lace curtains at the windows and make simple tiebacks from a cheerful chintz fabric.

✦ Consider hanging ruffled lace or chintz fabric behind glass cabinet doors to give your kitchen an English Victorian feeling.

✦ Place an extra shelf or two on a lonely wall, apply white paint or color wash, and fill with assorted china and crystal.

✦ Place a tall handmade broom in the corner for use and for show.

✦ Some kitchens have plenty of space for a comfortable easy chair, slipcovered in a shabby chic style. Try an overscale cabbage rose pattern; it promises to be as at home in an English country kitchen as in the parlor.

✦ Flower arrangements should be informal, loose, and mixed. A pretty white ironstone pitcher makes the perfect container.

✦ The English have a penchant for eclectic collectibles placed informally throughout their country homes. It's never too much when the objects are special and tastefully arranged.

✦ Look for decorative accessories that double as serving pieces and kitchen utensils–everything from old painted boxes for toothpicks to Wedgwood teapots used to hold fresh-cut flowers from the garden.

✦ An iron cauldron and old oversized pots are reminiscent of "Upstairs, Downstairs" and times past, when the kitchen staff was sizeable and the guests were numerous. Fill the big vessels with dried flowers or use them for a banquet!

✦ Bulletin boards can be decorative as well as useful, especially when you cover a piece of thin plywood with a pretty chintz or vintage floral fabric and then create a latticework design over your entire fabric area with lengths of elastic cut to "weave" over the surface–the plastic holds messages in place. Nail the elastic strips to the back of the bulletin board. It's a perfect place for helpful reminders, souvenir postcards, greeting cards, and thoughtful notes from friends.

✦ If you're considering wallpaper (always a great tool for change), look for a motif that doesn't necessarily scream "kitchen." An elegant botanical or other print meant for a dining room could also be stylish in the kitchen. Stripes and ticking designs can make a low-ceilinged kitchen look larger. You may want to experiment with floral designs that have the feeling of an English garden. But before you invest in dozens of rolls of a design you've just fallen for, tape a large sample to one wall and live with it for a while.

American Country

✦ American folk art quickly establishes a characteristic look. Consider hanging a hooked rug on the wall (away from cooking odors, of course), placing a whimsical whirlygig on a country cupboard, using a spongeware bowl to hold shiny green apples, or arranging a wooden watermelon collection atop the counter.

✦ Braided throw rugs cushion those long hours spent chopping and mixing or doing a sink full of dishes. They're colorful, durable, and they shake clean. Be sure to use a thin skid pad underneath to prevent slipping, especially if your floors are tile or polished wood.

✦ Wrought-iron trivets–whether vintage originals or reproductions–can make an artistic statement when hung on the wall. To show off a handsome collection, hang large pieces of pegboard, paint them the color of the wall, and attach trivets with peg hooks. They're easy to remove and place in service. Single trivets can be hung by a long nail.

✦ Wreaths made of softly colored everlastings find a home in the American country kitchen. You might also try a simple grapevine wreath trimmed with a pretty plaid ribbon.

✦ A row of spongeware bowls is always fresh and appealing.

✦ Fish decoys painted in soft colors–found at antique shows and shops–are fitting art for the kitchen. Hang in a row, or make them swim across the wall.

✦ Dried herbs can be tied onto a hanging or standing rack along with dish towels made of homespun fabric. For party occasions in the kitchen, tie a small bunch of dried herbs on the back of each chair.

✦ Place a colorful old penny rug in the center of the kitchen table with an old-fashioned lazy Susan on top.

✦ Cooking utensils are easy to get to when they're stored in a decorative stoneware jug on the counter.

✦ Find the perfect oak rocker for your kitchen, and set it by a sunny window.

✦ Fill a wooden bucket with dried flowers and place it on the floor.

✦ Fake fruits and vegetables–*trompe l'oeil* objects made of wood, marble, ceramics, wax, or papier mâché–make lovely permanent arrangements.

◆ Use old checkerboards to make graphic wall art.

◆ Swag a country-check fabric across the tops of your kitchen windows.

◆ Rustic twig-style bar stools with animal-hide seats can turn any workstation into a western-style place to gather for a meal.

◆ Consider a brass candle chandelier in the kitchen. The romantic candle glow in the evening will transform your family dining area.

◆ Primitive country benches are as at home in the kitchen as they are in the rest of the house. A bench not only offers family and friends a place to drop their things and sit for a while, but also provides additional storage space underneath.

◆ Place or hang folk-art objects and American country antiques related to the kitchen on a shelf or window ledge: carved dolls and barnyard animals, old medicine bottles, decorative butter molds, or antique utensils.

◆ A floor cloth stenciled in a quilt or theorem painting design is both attractive and sensible in the American country kitchen.

◆ Cookbooks by the dozen become decorative objects in themselves. Stack them in a line, on a shelf, on a baker's rack, or use several oversized books as a pedestal upon which to set a lamp.

✦ American baskets are light, attractive, and always ready when arranged on top of kitchen cabinets or in the lower portion of open shelving.

✦ Here's an inspired new use for wonderful old flatware if your drawer handles or door pulls are worn or just plain dull. Have small holes drilled in antique knives, forks, and spoons–the odd bits of flatware found at tag sales and flea markets, rarely two of the same–to match up with the existing screw holes in your drawers or doors. Then remove the existing hardware and replace with your whimsical new pulls. Most silversmiths suggest looking

for flatware that is sturdy (avoid the more delicate patterns) so as to prevent the bending or loosening of handles. Wooden spoons provide a rustic variation on this clever idea.

✦ Begin looking for old graters and sieves at flea markets. Then hang them from your pot rack to add interest to the new things.

✦ An unusual and fanciful hanging lamp can be made from a tin colander–old, new, standard size, or chef's size. Select from several graphic punched designs (stars are fun), then run an electrical cord through a hole drilled in the top. Electrify

The kitchen is
    the heart of the home,
and the mother is
    queen of the kitchen.
        Owen Meredith (1921)

it using an adapter kit found at most hardware stores. Hang it by the cord from the ceiling and plug the cord into a wall outlet. You can also wind the cord through a metal chain.

◆ Painted watering cans are meant to be seen in the American country kitchen. You'll need them to water your many pots of herbs and ivy, of course!

◆ Because of their rare and fragile nature, old quilts and other antique textiles present a tricky question for kitchen use. A smart rule of thumb: seek the pretty yet truly "timeworn" textiles that have out-lived their collectible value but still have much to offer in terms of adornment and use. Then keep them away from heat, kitchen odors, and bright sunlight.

◆ It's reassuring somehow to keep a small light turned on in the kitchen after dark. Small table lamps with soft pink bulbs of fifty to eighty watts provide a cozy atmos-phere as well as supplemental light on gloomy days.

◆ You don't have to be a magician to use mirrors to expand a small kitchen. Try a pine mirror on a wall behind the kitchen table or have a long piece of mirror cut to fit the space under the kitchen cabinets. A grouping of whimsically framed small mirrors becomes a bright and artful arrangement on a dark wall.

◆ You'll be able to keep your children's so-called refrigerator artwork neat and clean for posterity if you buy inexpensive plexiglass clip frames. Choose a "gallery" wall and change the show frequently. This idea has many benefits. Children's artwork adds cheer and color, and your children will feel very important when you praise their work by framing it.

◆ Start a collection of cookware, utensils, linens or other items for the kitchen. Old salt and pepper shakers, for example, come in every imaginable motif from pink flamingos to wishing wells. They're bright, useful, novel, fun to display, and even more fun to find.

WREATHS FOR ALL SEASONS

In ancient times, crowns of oak and laurel leaves were placed on the heads of patriots, poets, warriors, and the like to honor them. This early wreath-making has made its way over the years into our home decorations and celebrations, symbolizing abundance and goodness.

What better spot to hang a wreath than in a kitchen? There's an exciting variety of natural herbs and spices as well as many fruits and vegetables that provide color, texture, and that friendly kitchen feeling. Since many kitchen wreath materials are edible–garlic, dried peppers, and bay leaves, for example–these wreaths are user-friendly, too.

There are numerous materials with which to create a base: try using grapevine, laurel, lemon leaves, wild rose hip, or wheat, barley, or oat sheaves. Smooth sumac makes a pretty base with its red berries, as does Stag Horn sumac, which is a deeper red and velvety in texture. Here are some ingredients for a variety of wreaths that perfectly suit the most popular room in the house–the kitchen.

◆ Fresh garlic from the grocery store works best when hot-glued with either the root or the stem showing.

◆ Bay leaves may be snapped off for use in soups and stews.

◆ Cinnamon sticks look pretty grouped in bunches with ribbons.

◆ Small fresh chili peppers air dry and add color.

◆ Dried pomegranates–the smaller ones work best–add a unique texture.

◆ Whole nutmeg can be scratched slightly with a kitchen grater to release the scent.

...More and more households will turn to the computer
    for invaluable assistance in food preparation
and kitchen management.
    What it can't do is come up with ideas...That's still up to us.

Julee Rosso & Sheila Lukins (1979)

+ Small, shiny pearl onions or shallots add texture.

+ Baby artichokes dry on the wreath.

+ Fruit slices–orange, lemon, grapefruit– should be pre-dried before being added to a wreath.

+ Chive flowers, when cut at the right moment, make especially pretty wreath decorations; the same is true for dill seed heads and mint flowers.

+ Clumps of pepperberries, which usually come from Canada or Florida, can be found in many flower markets.

+ Kumquats and lady apples are wonderful for Christmas wreaths, and will last through the holidays.

+ Look for okra pods and poppy seed pods at your flower market.

+ Miniature pumpkins and ears of corn are perfect for fall arrangements; the tiny pumpkins will last six months to a year and can be attached with a wooden pick.

+ Familiar kitchen herbs, such as fresh mint, dry very well; also try purple basil (it must be the dark variety, such as opal or purple ruffles), thyme, and sage. It's a pleasure to pluck cooking herbs from your wreath and savor the scent.

+ Used in Earl Grey tea, bee balm leaves are worth the search to add to a wreath. Nigella pod–also called love-in-a-mist–is a tan oval pod with a wine-colored stripe that is sometimes found at flower markets; it's used to flavor string cheese.

◆ Sunflower heads are pretty and the seeds are delicious.

◆ Look for freeze-dried fruits and vegetables, such as tiny potatoes and papaya halves; they add an unusual touch to a kitchen wreath.

◆ Most natural wreath decorations can be easily attached to the base with a hot glue gun, toothpicks, florist's wire, string, or ribbon. Begin with the simple base and gradually build your signature wreath design as you find the perfect touches.

SHELF DRESS-UP IDEAS

Plain kitchen shelves can be trimmed in a variety of simple ways to please (and surprise) anyone who happens to open the cupboard door. Open shelving cries out for that extra decorative touch. The utilitarian spaces in your kitchen can easily take on new country character. Here are several ideas to get your kitchen shelves off to a pretty start.

◆ Tack narrow grosgrain ribbon, striped or solid, to the edge of the shelf. Coordinate with solid-colored shelf paper.

◆ Line shelves with cloth or paper doilies, lapping the lace over the shelf edge. Square doilies can be placed on the diagonal so that their points provide a lace accent. Pretty napkins or pieces of vintage fabric can be handled in much the same way for instant charm. Secure the cloth napkins with bits of masking tape in the back and on the sides; use small white thumbtacks for the paper trimmings.

◆ Brass studs and tacks that come in a variety of designs are easy to apply. Check out the stars, the hearts, and the flowers. Create your own design pattern on shelf edge and door fronts as well.

◆ Decorative trims, such as braiding, fringe, upholstery tape, and ruffling, can be found at most sewing centers or in notions departments.

◆ Felt, which is easy to cut and smooth into position, is perfect for a tailored look.

✦ Accent by adding contrasting ribbon trim to the shelf edge. Try gray felt with red grosgrain ribbon or green felt with black-and-white plaid ribbon.

✦ Open shelving can be given an authentic, rustic look by applying interestingly shaped twigs to all the front edges. Use a hot glue gun, but before you start, make certain the look is right for you, as it's difficult to undo.

✦ For a striking band of color, paint the shelf edge a primary crayon-like color, jet black, or angelic gold.

✦ You might also sponge, stencil, or faux-finish the edge . . . and consider including the entire shelf.

✦ Other unusual ideas for shelf edging are dried macaroni or beans, beads, twine, and buttons. The sky's the limit!

✦ Another simple solution is wallpaper borders. Border the kitchen walls with the same pattern you've used on the shelves, or vice versa.

✦ Lace is always charming—a card of antique lace discovered in the attic, or something bought yesterday at the local variety store. Use small white thumbtacks at both ends, making sure your length of lace is drawn taut.

GIVING GIFTS FROM THE KITCHEN

A prettily wrapped jar of jam or a thoughtful tin of cookies is always appreciated as a gift—yet it is easy to go beyond these staples to create truly unique gifts from the kitchen that will be memorable.

✦ Lovingly worn pots and pans—with little chips, dents, and soft finishes that speak of countless home-cooked meals—are fun finds at garage sales and flea markets (not to mention that mellowed copper pot shoved to the back of your cookware shelf). They make wonderful containers in which to plant herbs—basil, thyme, sage, and oregano especially. If there are any small holes in the bottom of the pot, you'll need to either use it outdoors or place a tray beneath it. If there are no holes, be sure to place pebbles or bits of broken

crockery in the bottom for drainage before adding soil.

◆ It's time to give up that well-guarded family recipe, the one your great aunt Jane wrote out for you in longhand years ago and that your friends have been begging for. Make a color photocopy of the original (or recopy it on a special paper, such as laid-finish paper, rice paper, or even parchment). Then treat the recipe as art by floating it in a smart and simple glass or plexiglass frame. This heirloom recipe stands up handily on a shelf or counter, a reminder of your thoughtfulness.

◆ Keep a supply of attractive and inexpensive gift baskets in the top of a closet, ready to use at a moment's notice. When the occasion arises, arrange in a basket one of your best-loved recipes plus all the necessary ingredients to make it. For your favorite raspberry vinaigrette recipe, the basket would contain ingredients such as extra-virgin olive oil, a fine raspberry vinegar, Dijon mustard, a whole head of garlic, and a jar of fancy peppercorns.

◆ A variation on this notion is to mark a favorite recipe in a cookbook (place a pretty bookmark by the world's greatest chocolate-chip cookie recipe, for example). Then wrap the called-for ingredients together with the book in clear cellophane, using the book as a base, or place the whole thing in one of your baskets.

◆ A grand welcome-wagon gift for the neighborhood newcomer is a small kitchen corkboard on which are listed the names and addresses of nearby stores– the best grocery store, produce market, flower shop, gourmet market, butcher, fish market, etc. Add business cards from these establishments to help any newcomer get settled. A selection of menus from restaurants that provide take-out service is a thoughtful addition.

✦ Simple, time-tested, and always welcome gifts include long sticks of cinnamon tied with a bow, a bouquet of dried herbs, a string of garlic, a small bag filled with ginger root, or a mesh bag of shallots. If you keep plenty of ribbons in a basket and rolls of cellophane nearby, you'll never be hard pressed to come up with instant housewarming gift wrappings.

✦ Fill a glass mason jar, canister, or decorative tin with freshly roasted coffee beans. Into the aromatic beans, stick a coffee measuring spoon and a long-handled brush (an inexpensive paint or makeup brush will do) to brush out the coffee grinder. A note identifying the coffee is a nice touch. Don't forget to say if the coffee's decaf or the wide-eyed variety.

✦ A decorative mug or super-size tea cup is just waiting to be filled with a package of tea leaves and a strainer.

✦ The kitchen is a good "theme" for more practical gift ideas, such as a fun cleaning package: fill a brightly colored cleaning pail or roomy mesh bag with thin expandable sponges, good silver polish, a silver cloth, a tube of scented hand cream, and a pair of colorful rubber gloves. Then for fun, add a list of cleaning services to the gift assortment.

✦ No gift list would be complete without something for the busy working person who has little time in the kitchen. Fill a basket with a bottle of wine, a corkscrew, fancy paper plates and napkins, an all-purpose serving spoon–and a list of the best take-out spots in the neighborhood!

✦ Prepare a delicious dinner in a new ceramic casserole dish. Enclose a note that says the dish becomes the gift after dinner!

chapter two

The Well-Outfitted Kitchen

COOKWARE AND UTENSILS

The expansive cookware departments of stores can be exciting, if slightly over-whelming, especially if you're setting up a kitchen for the very first time. Every pot, pan, and fabulous gadget looks as though it could turn you into an instant four-star wonder, but putting together a complete kitchen and finding the mix of cook-ware that best suits an individual style and particular kitchen size and arrangement is what counts. Although every cook's needs are slightly different, there are basic requirements to keep in mind when it comes to kitchen equipment. There's no need to get fancy at the start; a simple list of assorted cooking and baking items is a good foundation. Remember to invest in quality rather than quantity. You can always add a chef's knife or two or an expensive omelet pan later.

FOR STOVETOP AND OVEN

Select good-quality cookware that absorbs and transfers heat well. Your choices include various grades of the following materials: stainless steel, enameled steel, aluminum clad with a layer of stainless steel, cast iron, enamel on cast iron, aluminum, and copper. It's a good idea to investigate the pros and cons of each before making this important kitchen investment.

3 saucepans: 2-quart; 3- or 3½-quart; 5-quart; all with lids

2 frying pans: small (6" or 8" in diameter) and large (10" or 12" in diameter.) The larger frying pan will be suitable for your rapid browning or frying. Consider the benefits of non-stick pans.

1 12" sauté pan with lid

1 large kettle or stock pot: 8- 10-quart with lid

1 roasting pan: 17" x 11" x 3"

2 casseroles: 3-quart round with cover; 6-quart oval with cover

FOR BAKING

2 round cake pans: 8" or 9" in diameter, 1½" deep

1 rectangular cake pan: 13" x 9" x 2"

2 wire cooling racks

1 round pie plate: 9" in diameter and 1½" deep, glass or metal

1 loaf pan: approximately 9" x 5" x 3", glass or metal

2 baking sheets

1 12-cup muffin tin, standard size

FOR ALL YOUR MEASURING, MIXING, AND PREPARATION NEEDS

Baster

Cheese grater

Chopping board

Colander

Corkscrew

Flour sifter: 5-cup size

Garlic press

Grater, four-sided standing

Ice cream scoop

Kitchen shears

Kitchen timer

Ladle

Liquid measuring cup: choose a heavy-duty glass measuring cup that is heat resistant

Dry measuring cups: choose a set in graduated sizes

Measuring spoons: select good quality with deep bowls

Meat thermometer

Metal utensils for mixing and cooking: spoon, slotted spoon, spatula (A plastic spatula is needed for non-stick pans.)

Mixing bowls: choose a graduated nest in glass, stainless steel, or ceramic

Oven thermometer

Pasta scoop

Pastry blender

Pastry brush

Pepper and salt mills; or a combination mill

Potato peeler

Rolling pin: heavy 14" to 16" size

Rubber spatula

Sieves: a fine mesh strainer basket and a larger wire sieve

Tongs: wooden or metal

Wire whisk: buy at least one 8" or 10"

Wooden spoons: you'll want several in the 10" or 12" size

SMALL EQUIPMENT FOR THE KITCHEN

Coffee grinder

Coffee maker

Electric can opener

Electric hand mixer

Food processor

Knife sharpening stone (or an electric knife sharpener)

Toaster

KNIVES FOR CUTTING, CHOPPING, AND SLICING

Good quality sharp knives are absolutely essential for every cook. The first five knives in this list are the basics that belong in every kitchen; you may want to add the others at a later date.

3- or 3½" paring knife for light jobs

5" utility knife

Wide 8" chef's knife for chopping

10" serrated bread knife

10" chef's knife for slicing

10" ham or roast slicer

Cleaver

Boning knife

ALWAYS NICE TO HAVE

Bottle stoppers

Canisters, tins, or mason jars for staples

Copper mixing bowl for beating egg whites

Electric frying pan

Garlic cellar

Herb mill

Jar gripper: rubber

Lemon reamer

Lemon zester

Melon baller

Mini muffin tin

Omelet pan

Pastry board

Pot watcher: this is a glass disk that keeps pots from boiling over

Salad spinner

Tea strainer

Vegetable mandoline

Wok

Once your kitchen is stocked with good basic equipment, you can add and upgrade over the years to suit your changing needs.

A thoughtful idea: include this list with a kitchen shower gift.

DEFINING DINNERWARE: FORMAL AND EVERYDAY

Each day we stack ceramics in our cupboards and set them on our tables, taking them for granted. Whether we own our grandmother's heirloom gold-trimmed china, are registering a floral pattern we love at a bridal registry, or are simply adding to that utilitarian white dishware that has served our active family for years, it's important to understand what we own and what we may one day acquire. Making decisions about dinnerware based on individual need plus knowledge is the basis for good choices that last.

Here is the beautiful world of ceramics defined, from the popular and easily recognized to the rare and unusual. This concise glossary provides most of the definitions a person needs to get started– and then some.

Bone china: A type of porcelain made with the addition of bone ash, which is pure white in color.

Ceramics: A nineteenth-century term covering porcelain and all types of pottery.

China: Also called porcelain–a hard, dense, white substance made of white China clay that is translucent, impermeable, and resonant when struck.

Chinese export porcelain: China that was exported to the west between the sixteenth and nineteenth centuries in response to an overwhelming desire for Chinese porcelain in Europe and North America.

Creamware: An earthenware developed during the eighteenth century that is glazed with liquid lead. This pottery is pale yellow in color and fired at a low temperature. It is dangerous to eat from dishes that have a lead glaze, but modern reproductions are lead-free and perfectly safe.

Delftware: A Dutch tin-glazed earthenware (often blue and white) made during the eighteenth century to imitate more expensive Chinese porcelains.

Earthenware: Pottery made of a baked red clay. There are many types of earthenwares, but all, unless glazed, are porous.

Faience: French earthenware pottery with opaque glazes made from tin oxide.

Flow blue: Created by mistake circa 1820 when an English potter allowed ammonia to mix with blue cobalt-oxide decoration before final glazing. During firing the design bled, creating a flowing effect. Marketed primarily as dinnerware, flow blue is made with a white ironstone base, which is semi-porcelain.

Graniteware: A lightweight, enamel-coated cookware made of steel. Graniteware was first introduced at the 1876 Centennial Exposition in Philadelphia. Manufacturers offered this cookware in many solid colors, as well as with granite-like markings.

Hard paste porcelain: The equivalent of true porcelain. It is made of a nonporous white china clay called kaolin that is then combined with other substances. It is known for its strength and hardness.

Haviland: Fine porcelain tableware made for the American market in Charles Haviland's factory in Limoges, France.

Imari: Japanese porcelain adorned with bright floral patterns, as well as scenic designs, in blue, red, and gold. Handpainted Imari was specifically made for export.

Ironstone: A very tough, nontranslucent earthenware, patented in 1813 by Charles James Mason and produced in America and England.

Ironstone china: A very tough, porcelain-like substance made by adding glassy ironstone slag to the usual hard porcelain. Made exclusively by Staffordshire until 1827, and later produced throughout England and North America.

Jasperware: Characterized by light figures on a darker background, this is a type of earthenware developed by Josiah Wedgwood.

Lusterware: Dinnerware decorated by applying different colored lusters to clay bodies to achieve a metallic luster in imitation of silver, gold, and copper.

Majolica: Italian earthenware covered with an opaque tin glaze; sculptural in form and colorfully decorated.

Meissen: Founded in 1710, Meissen was the first porcelain manufacturer. The company is best known for its figures and enamel painting.

Minton: A Staffordshire company that produced fine earthenwares and bone china.

Mochaware: An earthenware with a name derived from its vivid, decorative patterns which resemble the markings of a mochastone, a type of agate found near the Arabian port of Mocha. Antique mochaware was made primarily for use in taverns.

Pearlware: A whiter form of creamware developed by Wedgwood, usually used for transfer printing.

Porcelain: Originating between the seventh and eighth centuries in China, porcelain is another term for china.

Pottery: A term used to describe items of baked clay that without their glaze would be porous. The clay may be sunbaked or fired in kilns at high temperatures. The color depends on the elements in the clay.

Redware: A fragile earthenware made from a number of clays ranging in color from tan to red or sometimes black. Redware is fired to a red color and glazed. It is porous and very sensitive to extreme temperatures.

Soft paste porcelain: An imitation of true porcelain that is fired at a lower temperature and decorated with enamels.

Spongeware: Any pottery whose surface patterns have been created by applying the glaze with a sponge or fabric swab. Color combinations include the rare green-on-white or the more common blue-on-white, as well as tricolor layers of brown, green, and ocher.

When the western sun shone broad and merry
   over the sparkling window, yellow floor and white tables;
when a savor of sweet marjoram and lavender from the
   window boxes was in the air and the shining stove with its
   bright teakettle and simmering pans was a shrine of good cheer,
I have taken portfolio and books out into my kitchen to the
   lightstand and little Shaker chair to enjoy the sparkling humor,
   the warm home radiance, the neatness and seemliness which
   made the place akin to poetry and clear thoughts.

Mrs. S. D. Powers (1884)

Staffordshire: Producer of both pottery and porcelain at the center of English ceramic production.

Stone china: A stoneware developed in the early nineteenth century by Spode made with china stone.

Stoneware: A hard, dense, and resonant pottery that fires to tan or light gray. This nonporous, opaque pottery is made from a mixture of clay and feldspar, a hardening mineral. Salt glazed stoneware is created by throwing salt into the fire of a kiln in which pots are being baked, producing a glaze with a slightly pitted surface.

Transferware: Ceramics made when a copper plate is engraved with a design, inked with a color glaze, and then printed onto tissue. The image on the tissue is then rubbed onto the object that is being decorated, soaked off, then fired to fix the desired design. Glazing is the final step.

Yellowware: An ovenproof pottery made from a variety of fine clays that fire to a color between light and dark yellow.

You don't need to be a collector to recognize a wonderful piece of antique majolica, or have breakfast at Tiffany's to select your first set of bone china. True appreciation of ceramics comes from understanding the fascinating and often amazing processes involved. This introduction should be just the beginning.

A Shopping List for a Well-Stocked Pantry

Every household has its own ideas about what a well-stocked pantry should hold. The following list is meant to be a good basic list for people who enjoy spending quality time in their kitchens. How nice to have everything an arm's reach away when friends drop by and you decide to pull together a delicious pasta dinner for six. Think of this list as your kitchen version of the famous Boy Scout motto, "Be prepared." If you keep the pantry stocked according to these basic principles, you'll be ready for anything.

It's a good idea to make a copy of this list and tape it on the back of the pantry door. Cross out and add according to your needs and taste. Soon you'll have a pantry list that is just right for your kitchen. (You might want to share it with a friend who loves to cook or a beginner in the kitchen who might like some advice.)

CHEESE

Parmesan: keep chunks in freezer and grate as needed

PASTA, RICE, AND BEANS

Dried or canned beans, such as black, kidney, pinto, and navy

Linguini (or another long type of dried pasta)

Rotini or ziti (or another small type of dried pasta)

White and brown rice

Wild rice

OILS

Olive oil–buy the best quality you can find, for this is a staple

Flavored olive oil–sprigs of rosemary, tarragon, or chunks of garlic

Sesame oil

Vegetable oil

VINEGARS

Balsamic–both dark and white

Cider–flavored with any of the following: garlic, peppercorns, basil, tarragon, rosemary, dill

Novelty—raspberry, peach, blueberry

Red wine

Rice wine

White wine

MUSTARDS

Dijon

Herbed–with green peppers, tarragon, or basil

Grainy–in crocks

Honey

Plain American—yellow hot-dog type

CONDIMENTS

Anchovy paste (in tube)

Capers

Chutney

Horseradish

Hot pepper sauce

Soy sauce (light)

Steak sauce

Tomato paste (in tube)

Worcestershire sauce

BROTH

Purchase broths in cans or as bouillon cubes; buy the low-salt kind if you have health concerns

Beef

Chicken

Vegetable

DRIED FRUITS AND NUTS

Almonds

Apricots

Cranberries

Pecans

Raisins

Walnuts

DRIED HERBS AND SPICES

Basil

Bay leaf

Chili powder

Cinnamon

Cloves

Curry powder

Dill

Ginger

Nutmeg

Oregano

Parsley

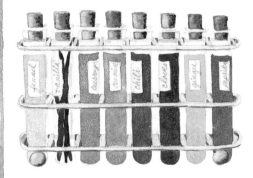

Peppercorns (black, white, and pink)

Rosemary

Salt

Tarragon

Thyme

FLAVORED EXTRACTS

Almond

Lemon

Vanilla

BAKING ESSENTIALS

Baking powder

Baking soda

Brown sugar

Chocolate chips

Confectioners' sugar

Cornmeal

Cornstarch

Corn syrup (light and dark)

Flour

Molasses

Granulated sugar

Food coloring

Unsweetened chocolate

Semisweet chocolate

Powdered cocoa

COFFEE

Regular and decaffeinated

Espresso–regular and decaffeinated

Flavored–almond, cinnamon, hazelnut, vanilla

TEAS

Apricot

Black currant

Chamomile

Earl Grey

English breakfast

Lemon or orange spice

Mint

Plum

Vanilla

CRACKERS

Bread sticks

Butter crackers

Seasoned crackers (poppy, sesame, onion)

Soda crackers

Wheat crackers

BEVERAGES

Tonic water

Mineral water

Sparkling mineral water or club soda

Bottled lemon juice and lime juice

LIQUOR

Vodka

Gin

Scotch

Rum

Bourbon

Liqueurs and cordials for drinking and cooking, including Kahlúa, Grand Marnier, and Calvados

Beer: domestic and imported

WINE

3 bottles of red

3 bottles of white

CANDLES

12-inch tapers in white or beige, gold, hunter green, bronze, and burgundy

Votive candles or tea lights

FLOWER ARRANGING SUPPLIES

Organize the pantry with buckets, vases, flower frogs, Spanish moss, white and black rocks, green and clear marbles, pine cones, driftwood, florist's wire, and Oasis. If friends arrive clutching a just-picked bunch of flowers, you'll be able to create a stunning arrangement on a moment's notice.

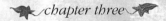
Exploring and Enjoying Your Pantry

UNDERSTANDING VINEGARS AND OLIVE OILS

Many of us are truly confused when confronted with the great (and growing) variety of vinegars and oils on the shelves of grocery and specialty stores. Once you understand the basics, you can experiment with confidence.

Vinegar

Vinegar is, quite simply, juice from a fruit that has fermented until it becomes acidic. The bases include many types of wines (reds, whites, Champagne, sherry); malted grains; and fruits and berries (pears, apples, raspberries, blackberries).

Vinegar is among the oldest elements in the cook's pantry; the Chinese used rice wine to make vinegar more than three thousand years ago, and the French have had their "sour wine" for eons. Following are definitions of some of the most common kinds of vinegars.

Distilled: Made by distilling alcohol from grains such as barley, corn, rye, or malt. Very acidic and best for pickling.

Wine: Wine fermented to the point of acidity. Excellent in flavor and mildness for salad dressing and sauces. Herbs, such as basil, tarragon, mint, and rosemary, to

name a few, are frequently added to the base to make fancy vinegars.

Fruit: Fermented fruit juice made from a wide and growing variety of fruits and berries. The flavor is fresh, often sweet, and distinctive. The widely used cider vinegar is made from apples.

Olive Oil

Olive oil, a precious and important staple in our pantries, is pressed from the fruit of olive trees that grow in countries with warm climates and sandy soil. The most popular oils come from Italy, France, Spain, and Greece. As a rule, Italian oil tends to be nutty, French oil fruity, Spanish oil intense, and Greek oil mild in taste but thicker than the rest; however, these lines often blur. The important thing is to find a taste that's right for you.

Always buy olive oil in a glass bottle, as plastic may pass its flavor to the oil. Store your olive oil in a cool, dark place but not in the refrigerator. Following are definitions of some of the most common kinds of olive oil.

Extra extra virgin or extra virgin: Made from the first pressing of the olives. Generally green to very dark green. This is the highest quality oil and has the most intense flavor.

Virgin: Usually the result of a second pressing. Sweet, nutty flavor.

Pure: Made from oils extracted from previously pressed olive pulp that has been treated with solvents.

Fine: Also extracted from olive pulp with water added. For cooking or frying only.

Light: Refined olive oil to which little or no extra-virgin is added; not lower in fat and calories.

Many oils are flavored with herbs such as basil, tarragon, garlic, and peppercorns. It's a good idea to buy one at a time and experiment with each one in different dressings and dishes. Note: Pour a quantity of olive oil into a plastic spray bottle and mist salads and foods before cooking.

AN ALPHABET OF HERBS

How many times have we stood in front of the endless little rows of herb jars and bottles in our cupboard, wondering just which one (or which combination) best suits the plain fish in the baking dish or the unseasoned beef cubes beginning to simmer on the stove? The following list guides you, from anise through thyme.

Anise: Carrots, chicken, cookies, fish, fruit, pork, spinach

Basil: Beef, broccoli, cabbage, carrots, cauliflower, eggplant, eggs, fish, green beans, lamb, pasta, pesto sauce, potatoes, poultry, rice, salad dressings, squash, spinach, tomatoes, veal

Bay leaf: Beef, chicken, fish, lamb, pâté, soups and stews, stocks, tomatoes, tomato sauce, veal

Borage: Chicken, fish, iced tea, salads, cold soups

Caraway: Beef, cabbage or sauerkraut, cauliflower, cheese, eggs, fish, green beans, peas, pork, potatoes, spinach, squash

Chervil: Carrots, chicken, corn, eggs, fish, peas, salads, spinach, tomatoes, veal

Chives: Asparagus, carrots, cauliflower, corn, eggs, fish, peas, potatoes, poultry, salads, soups, spinach, tomatoes, veal

Artur has his piano.
I play my sonatas on
the stove.

Nella Rubinstein (1957)

Clove: Cabbage, ham, mulled wine or cider, pickles

Coriander/Cilantro (coriander is the plant; cilantro is the leaf): Curries, eggs, fish, game, lamb, mushrooms, pâté, pickles, pork, potatoes, poultry, salsa, sauces, soups, tomatoes

Cumin: Beef, cabbage, carrots, cauliflower, chicken, curries, dried beans, lamb

Ginger: Beef, carrots, chicken, fish, fruit, lamb, pork, squash, veal

Lemongrass: Chicken, curries, fish, pork,soups

Lemon verbena: Chicken, fish, fruit, teas

Lovage: Meats, pâté, potatoes, poultry, soups, stews, stuffings, tomatoes

Marjoram: Beef, cabbage, carrots, cauliflower, eggplant, eggs, fish, green beans, lamb, mushrooms, pasta, poultry, sausages, squash, stuffings, tomatoes, veal

Mint: Carrots, desserts, dried beans, eggplant, fruit, green beans, lamb, peas, sauces, veal

Nutmeg: Fish, onions, pies, soups, white sauce

Oregano: Beef, broccoli, chicken, eggplant, eggs, fish, lamb, mushrooms, pasta, pork, potatoes, squash, tomatoes

Parsley: Practically everything! Beef, carrots, cauliflower, dried beans, eggplant, fish, lamb, potatoes, poultry, sauces, soups and stews, stuffings, tomatoes, veal

Rosemary: Beef, breads, eggs, fish, lamb, mushrooms, peas, pork, poultry, soups and stews, squash, stuffings, veal

Saffron: Chicken, corn, eggs, fish, lamb, pork, rice

Sage: Asparagus, beef, cabbage, carrots, corn, dried beans, eggplant, eggs, fish, game, green beans, pâté, pork, potatoes, poultry, squash, stuffings, tomatoes, veal

Savory (summer and winter): Asparagus, beef, cabbage, carrots, cauliflower, eggplant, eggs, fish, game, green beans, peas, poultry, sausage, squash, tomatoes, veal

Tarragon: Asparagus, beef, broccoli, carrots, cauliflower, chicken, eggs, fish, lamb, mushrooms, peas, potatoes, rice, salad dressings, sauces, tomatoes

Thyme: Asparagus, beef, broccoli, carrots, corn, dried beans, eggplant, eggs, fish, game, green beans, lamb, mushrooms, peas, potatoes, poultry, rice, spinach, stuffings, tomatoes, veal

THE INTERNATIONAL COOK: HERBS AROUND THE WORLD

The sweet aroma of fresh basil in a pesto sauce, the unmistakable pungency of garlic in baked clams, the spicy taste of a curry that brings tears of joy—every ethnic cuisine has its own special flair. With a very basic knowledge of the herbs that best suit certain cuisines, provided in the list below, your kitchen will soon become a small United Nations of culinary triumph.

Cajun: Basil, bay leaf, black pepper, cayenne, garlic, thyme

Chinese: Anise (star), chili peppers, coriander, fennel, garlic, ginger root, pepper (white and black)

French: Bay leaf, fennel, garlic, lemon verbena, parsley, sorrel, tarragon, thyme

German: Anise, bay, caraway, dill

Indian: Cardamom, cayenne, coriander, cumin, fennel, garlic, ginger root, lemongrass, mint, saffron

Italian: Basil, bay leaf, chives, garlic, fennel, Italian (flat-leaf) parsley, oregano, rosemary, thyme

Mexican: Cayenne, coriander, cumin, garlic, oregano

Spanish: Basil, cilantro, cumin, garlic, saffron, thyme

MAKING A FOUR-STAR BOUQUET GARNI

Bouquet garni (pronounced boo-KAY gar-NEE) is simply a tiny bouquet or bundle of dried herbs tied up in a bit of cheesecloth and used to flavor stews, soups, and other simmering dishes. Long favored by the great cooks of the world, the bouquet garni is a kitchen essential–it also makes a wonderful gift.

The art of making and using a bouquet garni need not be a well-kept secret. Many kitchen shops sell gauze pouches that can be gathered tightly at the top using a string tie. The pouch is filled with dried or fresh herbs to suit the dish and, happily, there is no set or "right" combination of herbs. It all depends on what you're cooking and the flavor you wish to achieve. When the pouch is filled, the string is pulled tight and the bouquet garni is dropped into the simmering pot. The string should be long so that the tiny pouch can be removed easily when the dish is cooked. The dish will be fully flavored but without any visible evidence of herbs in the smooth stew or soup.

If you're unable to find a pre-made pouch, it's easy to make your own. Just cut clean cheesecloth into a small square, then fill with herbs and fasten at the top with string, or simply leave enough fabric to tie the top into a knot.

Here are three classic combinations - for your kitchen or as a gift for someone else's–to get you off to a savory start. The amounts depend on your seasoning sensibilities.

Southern France Flavor: A deep, rich mix of thyme, rosemary, marjoram, and savory

French Classic Mélange: A piquant mix of thyme, bay leaf, parsley, onion, marjoram, and pepper

For Seafood: A pungent mix of thyme, bay leaf, parsley, basil, fennel, and caraway

Tip: For a delicious hot mulled cider or wine, make a bouquet garni featuring whole cloves and cinnamon sticks.

YEAR-ROUND GARDEN HERBS

Here's a useful and simple way to freeze garden herbs to have them all winter long.

✦ In a food processor, purée fresh, cleaned herbs–such as basil, savory, dill, and mint, with the stems removed—in a small amount of water. Experiment by adding water as you process the mixture so that you have a thick, mushy liquid.

✦ Pour mixture into ice cube trays. Freeze.

✦ When frozen solid, pop out the cubes into freezer bags or plastic containers and store in the freezer.

✦ Your frozen herb cubes are handy for tossing into soups, stews, and other simmering dishes that require herbal flavors.

PEPPER TALK

A thousand or more years ago, pepper was so rare and treasured for its irresistible aroma that it was frequently used instead of money as fair trade. The various exotic names associated with certain peppers come from early pepper ports in India and the far east: Tellicherry, Alleppey, and Pandjang, for example. Whatever the names mean, it's fun to expand your pantry's pepper "vocabulary" with a variety of wonderful peppercorns to grind fresh into your everyday cooking.

In the fullest and best sense,
   how great is the significance of the term
   "a good housekeeper"!
Whether she rule in mansion or cottage,
   her sway must be over a household
   in which the chief element of a happy
   home will not be lacking.

Fannie Merritt Farmer (1914)

Are you looking for an aromatic pepper for that boned chicken breast, or something spicier for a fresh filet of sole? Before you reach for the pepper mill, know something about your choices. You'll find exciting new ways to cook with pepper, including adding a pinch of black pepper to your homemade pumpkin pie filling to enhance its other spices.

Black peppercorns: Probably the most familiar, this type of pepper has the strongest bite. The pepper berries are picked while still underripe, then dried. The entire berry is ground.

White peppercorns: The milder, deeply aromatic flavor and color makes these peppercorns especially well suited to cream and white sauces. The white color comes from using just the inside kernels, vine ripened before harvesting and soaked in water before the drying process.

Green peppercorns: A good choice if you're looking for a wonderfully mild flavor. They tend to be softer than the rest and are used whole. Delicious used in a mustard-type vinaigrette.

Pink peppercorns: These bright berries are a relatively recent addition to pepper mélanges. True pink peppercorns are the fully ripe berries, although many that are sold commercially come from a different, unrelated plant: the pepper tree. They add color and a sweet flavor.

JAVA TALK

Stores that specialize in coffee and coffee products–not to mention trendy coffee bars–are springing up in big cities and small towns alike. But the variety of products and flavors available can be daunting, so it's useful to learn about the many interesting coffee choices available now. This list is intended to simplify your choices so you can sit back and relax over that next great cup of coffee.

Columbian: The popular coffee from South America that we've become accustomed to reaching for on the shelf at the grocery store is rich and has a relatively mild flavor. Columbian is frequently blended with other coffees.

Costa Rican: This Central American country offers an excellent strong yet richly flavored coffee.

French or Italian roast: This coffee is easily distinguished by the glossy dark beans. Its full espresso flavor makes it a pleasing coffee to serve with dessert.

Hawaiian Kona: This coffee tends to be milder and sweeter, yet full and rich at the same time.

Mocha Java: A blend of two types of full and rich coffee beans: java and mocha.

Puerto Rican: Not as easily available, but this is a fine coffee when you can find it.

Vienna roast: If you're looking for a mild espresso, something lighter than French or Italian, then this one may be for you.

Jamaican Blue Mountain and High Mountain Supreme: These two coffees are up there in the rare and very expensive category because of their sweet, full-bodied flavors and their limited growing range.

House blend: Generally a coffee maker, grocery store, or coffee shop has developed a winning combination of beans that it enjoys passing along to its customers.

Ask first about its special characteristics. Then try it and see for yourself.

How to Make a Great Cup of Coffee

The cardinal rule in making a great cup of coffee: Make sure your beans are fresh. Never use inferior beans; your taste buds will know the difference.

✦ Use cold, fresh tap water, filtered tap water, or bottled spring water.

✦ Your equipment should always be clean and free of oils and residue.

✦ Know the correct grind–coarse to fine—for your particular type of brewing equipment.

On Cooking and Servants:
  She gets drunk once in a while,
  but men drink for less cause
  than cooking.

  Haryot Holt Cahoon (1893)

Can choice and costly dainties
taste more sweet
Than simple ones by honest
labour earned?

Fannie Merritt Farmer (1914)

◆ Invest in a good coffee scoop and measure your coffee with care.

◆ Generally, 2 level tablespoons per 6-ounce cup is recommended. (A 2-tablespoon scoop of coffee beans is equal to approximately the same measure when ground.) Some people add an extra scoop for strength.

◆ Never let freshly brewed coffee sit for longer than twenty minutes. There is no substitute for a cup of fresh coffee.

Make your own designer coffee by adding a pinch of cinnamon to the ground coffee before brewing; alternatively, a dash of unsweetened chocolate powder makes for a nice touch. More adventurous souls may want to try adding a piece of vanilla bean to taste.

THE PERFECT POT OF TEA

It's no wonder that tea is among the world's most popular beverages. The plant from which tea is made, *Camellia sinensis,* was first cultivated in China in prehistoric times. Tea soon spread throughout the Orient, and was exported to Europe in the early seventeenth century. It soon became practically a national obsession in Britain, and its tremendous popularity played a significant part in the opening of the Orient to western commerce.

Justly famous for its flavor, a cup of tea is also beloved for offering a brief respite during a busy day. Let your prettiest teapot sit right out on the kitchen counter to remind you to break for this relaxing ritual. A decorative and well-insulated tea cozy is a nice touch, and it also keeps your tea piping hot.

How to Make a Perfect Pot of Tea

✦ Select loose tea instead of tea bags for its more robust flavor and luscious aroma.

✦ Fill a kettle with fresh, cold tap water. Just before it comes to a full boil, pour a bit of water into the waiting teapot, swirl it around inside to warm the pot, then pour it out.

✦ Add loose tea leaves to the pot. (Some people prefer to use a diffuser or place the leaves in a small sieve or strainer that sits over the pot's opening.) Use one full teaspoonful per cup plus one "for the pot."

✦ Pour in boiling water and stir. Let the tea steep for at least five to ten minutes.

✦ Pour and enjoy. (If the tea is loose, pour through a fine strainer.)

✦ Spiced tea is delicious served with a cinnamon stick and honey.

✦ A real treat is tea with a tablespoon of orange liqueur.

✦ Shortbread or biscuits are always a welcome accompaniment.

Note: Herbal teas have taken over the store shelves! Here's a list of possible choices to ponder and try: Anise, Anise hyssop, Basil (especially Cinnamon basil), Bee balm, Borage, Catnip, Chamomile, Fennel seed, Horehound, Hyssop, Lemon balm, Lemongrass, Lemon verbena, Marjoram and Sweet marjoram, Mexican mint marigold, Oregano, Parsley, Pineapple sage, and Thyme.

chapter four

Natural Cleaning and Clever Storing

QUICK-FIX CLEANING TIPS FROM THE PANTRY

There's a tiny wad of chewing gum decorating your family room carpet after your seven-year-old's birthday bash. You grab your wallet and head out to find a cleaning remedy. Well, stop and look around at home first! Your food storage shelves contain some of the easiest and most environmentally healthy cleaning supplies you can find to help halt the damage. In this case, apply ice to the spot: as it chills, the sticky gum should loosen and lift off. Or, believe it or not, a tiny dab of peanut butter can help lift the gum. You may need a professional product to make your carpet look like new again, but these tips can keep things under control.

"What does cooking mean?"

It means the patience of Job and the persistence of the Pilgrim Fathers.

It means the endurance, the long-suffering, and the martyrdom
of Joan of Arc.

It means the steaming and the stewing and the baking and the
broiling, thrice daily, spring and summers and autumns and winters,
year after year, decade after decade.

It means perspirations and desperations and resignation.

It means a crown and a harp and a clear title to an estate in heaven.

Haryot Holt Cahoon (1893)

No one claims that items in the pantry can replace all your professional cleaning supplies, but there are easy natural remedies that can certainly help if company's coming and you need a quick fix for anything from spotty stainless steel to clothing stains.

✦ Vinegar has many uses beyond salad dressing. Cleaning glass is one of them. White vinegar has long been a traditional remedy for smudged and greasy windows. Run vinegar through the coffee maker to remove stains.

✦ Likewise, if you're washing fine crystal by hand, add a capful of white vinegar to the dishwater and your crystal will sparkle.

✦ For water spots on stainless steel, dampen a soft cloth with white vinegar and rub. Then wipe dry.

✦ Clogged shower heads? Remove and soak in a solution of half water and half vinegar overnight. By morning, most of the build-up should be a thing of the past. Rinse heads and replace.

◆ Vinegar is also helpful in taking care of that detergent build-up in the washing machine. With the setting on hot, add a half cup vinegar to the water. Use vinegar sparingly and infrequently, as the acidity could eventually damage washing machine parts.

◆ Baking soda has long been a wonderful way to keep your refrigerator free from unpleasant odors. Make sure the top of the box is open halfway, place the box in the refrigerator, and replace it every six months. To avoid tipping over the box, place it on a small plate and shove it to the back.

◆ To clean an aluminum percolator, fill the pot with water and add a handful of baking soda plus 1-3 teaspoons of cream of tartar. Run through one full cycle. Let cool and scrub with a non-abrasive pad, such as nylon netting.

◆ Renew the sparkle on chrome with a paste made of baking soda and water. Apply a thin coat to the chrome object. Let it dry and buff off with a clean cloth.

◆ Lemon juice mixed with salt helps perk up copper.

◆ Clean up brass with a dab of catsup right from the bottle.

◆ When the kids come home with grass-stained T-shirts and clothes, put white corn syrup on the stains as you would a pre-wash stain remover. Rinse. Repeat if your child has managed to bring home half the lawn!

◆ Club soda is a favorite natural cleaner for many unfortunate little accidents (including red wine) on clothing, carpeting, and upholstery. The good thing about treating spots with club soda is that it rarely leaves a telltale cleaning sign. In the absence of club soda, try mixing a little paste of water and salt.

◆ Check out the bottom of your glass coffee pot. If you see crusty little burned spots, pour a little table salt into the pot, add a small amount of water, and let stand. The salt helps loosen the crust so you can simply wash it out.

◆ Find a white water spot on your good end table? Dab on a bit of mayonnaise with a soft dry cloth and rub. This treatment may need to be repeated a few times if the spot has set.

◆ To help remove wrinkles from freshly-washed sheer curtains, put heavy dinner knives in the hems and hang to dry while still damp. The weight of the knives helps eliminate a long stand at the ironing board.

CLEVER KITCHEN KEEPERS

If you're tired of having your nice kitchen look like a grocery store with detergent bottles and cracker boxes in clear view, it's time for creative solutions. There are clever ways to store staples as well as other frequently used kitchen things in the open with style.

◆ Find the perfect spot for a small decorative garden urn, preferably near the kitchen table. Line it with a large napkin or a stack of folded napkins, then fill it with your flatware for easy reach. Or roll settings of flatware in cloth napkins (a floral design would be appropriate) and place them upright in the urn.

◆ Painted tin sap buckets make light and unusual holders for paper napkins. Grab a handful of napkins and roll slightly to fit the curve.

◆ An old fishing creel can be hung on the wall or set on a counter. With its lid up, it's a handy place to store your fancy vinegars and oils in the open.

◆ A cut-glass or etched cruet makes a pretty dishwashing liquid holder.

◆ Store your dish towels rolled in an oval wooden Shaker box without the top.

◆ A lovely ceramic soup tureen is the perfect cache for all those crackers that don't get put back in their proper boxes. To insure freshness, place the crackers in plastic storage bags. Then pop the bags in the tureen and replace the top. It's the perfect dry spot–till someone calls "Soup's on!"

✦ Store your kitchen utensils in a pottery mug or jug–or in a whole row of mugs in assorted shapes and sizes.

✦ Fancy homemade vinegars in attractive etched-glass bottles should sit right out in the open on a shelf or a counter.

✦ Fill empty spice bottles with sugar and cinnamon for shaking on French toast. These attractive little bottles are also good for holding flour to dust meats or fish before frying, for holding powdered sugar to dust cakes and cookies, or for holding toothpicks that shake out when needed.

✦ Everyone manages to collect small plastic grocery bags. Instead of stuffing them behind the refrigerator or in a crowded drawer, fold and pack them into an empty tissue box covered in pretty self-stick paper. Then pull out them as needed.

✦ Can't remember to take your vitamins in the morning? Place a small glass vase arranged with flowers in the center of a very fancy tray–perhaps silver or tole-work. Then surround the flowers with the family's vitamin bottles and they'll be sitting pretty for a change.

✦ Long narrow baskets are wonderful holders and separators for chopsticks, small cheese knives, bottle stoppers and all those miscellaneous kitchen items that get lost in a big drawer.

✦ Shaker pegboards and iron hooks can be placed in strategic spots in most kitchens to hold aprons, potholders, and dish towels.

✦ Looking for a permanent place for a spice chart? Invest in an attractively illustrated version and have it framed for the kitchen. You'll never again have to wonder if tarragon is right for that French dish.

✦ In lieu of the standard soap dish and rubber sponge holder, try placing a decorative ceramic dish by the sink–perhaps a blueware design or something in a wild red. Many pretty accessories sold for the bathroom can also dress up the kitchen.

HANDY CHARTS

Freezer Storage Limits

It's best to use frozen foods long before their expiration date to insure taste and freshness. For foods that require thawing before cooking or serving, refrigerator thawing is the best method. It takes longer but the food keeps better. Use thawed food immediately before quality and flavor begin to deteriorate.

Frozen Food Limits

FOOD	MAXIMUM STORAGE TIME
Meat	
Fresh Beef	**6-12 months**
Fresh veal, lamb	**6-9 months**
Fresh pork	**3-6 months**
Ground beef, veal and lamb	**3-4 months**
Ground pork	**1-3 months**
Variety meats	**3-4 months**
Wild game	**6 months**
Poultry	
Chicken-whole	**6-12 months**
Chicken-cut up	**6 months**
Turkey	**6 months**
Duck, goose-whole	**6 months**

Here's all the Forms of every
Implement to work or
carve with; so he makes
thee able
To deck the Dresser, and
adorn the Table.
And so you're welcome, pray
fall to, and eat.

Robert May (1667)

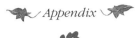

Fish

Fillets of lean fish	**4 months**
Fillets of fat fish	**3 months**
Shellfish	**2-4 months**
Cooked fish	**1-3 months**
Vegetables	**8-10 months**
Fruits	**8-12 months**
Fruit Juice Concentrates	**8-12 months**
Ice Cream and Sherbet	**1 month**
Herbs	**6 months**

Cookery is become an art,
a noble science.

Robert Burton,
1621

Tell me what you eat,
and I will tell you what
you are.

Anthelme Brillat-Savarin,
1825

U.S. MEASURES

Liquid Measures
3 tsp = 1 tbsp
2 pints = 1 liquid quart
4 tbsp = ¼ cup
4 quarts = 1 liquid gallon
5-⅓ tbsp = ⅓ cup

Dry Measures
12 tbsp. = ¾ cup
8 quarts = 1 peck
16 tbsp = 1 *
4 pecks = 1 bushel
2 cups = 1 pint
1 pound = 16 ozs

Equivalents

FOOD	WEIGHT	EQUIVALENT
Almonds, unshelled, whole	1 lb	1-$\frac{3}{4}$ cups nutmeats
Almonds, blanched, whole	1 lb	3-$\frac{1}{2}$ cups nutmeats
Apples (3 med)	1 lb	3-$\frac{1}{2}$ cups pared or sliced
Apricots	1 lb	3 cups dried; 6 cups cooked
Bananas (3 med)	1 lb	2 to 2-$\frac{1}{2}$ cups sliced
Beans, kidney, dried (2-$\frac{1}{3}$ cups)	1 lb	9 cups cooked
Beans, lima or navy, dried (2-$\frac{1}{3}$ cups)	1 lb	6 cups cooked
Beans, lima in pod	1 lb	$\frac{2}{3}$ cup shelled
Beets (4 med)	1 lb	2 cups diced and cooked
Bread	1 slice	$\frac{1}{4}$-$\frac{1}{3}$ cup dry crumbs
Bread	1 slice	$\frac{3}{4}$-1 cup soft crumbs
Butter (or margarine) stick	4 oz $\frac{1}{4}$ lb	8 tbsp
Butter (or margarine)	1 lb	2 cups (or 32 tbsp)
Cabbage	1 lb	3 cups shredded
Candied Fruit and Fruit Peels	$\frac{1}{2}$ lb	1-$\frac{1}{2}$ cups cut up
Carrots (8 to 10)	1 lb	2-$\frac{3}{4}$ cups sliced or diced
Celery (2 med bunches)	1 lb	4 cups diced
Cheese, cream	3 ozs	6 tbsp
Cheese, hard	1 lb	4 cups grated
Chicken	3-$\frac{1}{2}$ lbs	2 cups cooked and diced
Chocolate, unsweetened	1 square	1 oz (1 tbsp melted, 5 tbsp grated)
Cornmeal	1 cup uncooked	4 cups cooked
Crackers, graham	15	1 cup fine crumbs
Crackers, soda	22	1 cup fine crumbs
Cranberries	1 lb	4 cups

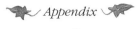

Cream, heavy (1 cup)	¹/₂ pint	2 cups whipped
Dates	1 lb	2 cups pitted
Egg Whites	8-11	1 cup
Egg Yolks	12-16	1 cup
Figs	1 lb	2-³/₄ to 3 cups chopped
Flour, all-purpose	1 lb	4 cups sifted
Flour, cake	1 lb	4-¹/₂ cups sifted
Garlic	1 med clove	¹/₄ tsp chopped
Gelatin	¹/₄ oz envelope	1 tbsp
Lemon or Lime	1 med	3-4 tbsp juice
Lemon, rind	1 med	1-¹/₂ to 2 tsp grated
Macaroni	1 cup (¹/₄ lb)	2 cups cooked
Meat	1 lb	2 cups diced
Milk, evaporated	14-¹/₂ oz can	1-²/₃ cups
Milk, sweetened, condensed	14 oz can	1-¹/₄ cups
Mushrooms, fresh	¹/₂ lb	2-¹/₂ cups sliced
Noodles (uncooked)	1 cup	1-³/₄ to 2 cups cooked
Onions	1 med	¹/₃ cup chopped
Orange	1 med	¹/₃ cup juice
Orange, rind	1 med	2 tbsp grated
Peanuts, unshelled	1 lb	2 to 2-¹/₂ cups nutmeats
Peas, in pod	1 lb	1 cup shelled and cooked
Peas, split	1 lb	2 cups
Pecans, unshelled	1 lb	2-¹/₄ cups nutmeats
Potatoes (3 potatoes)	1 lb	2-¹/₂ cups sliced or diced; 2 cups mashed
Prunes, dried	1 lb	2-¹/₂ cups; 4 cups cooked
Raisins	1 lb	3 cups
Rice, raw (¹/₂ lb)	1 cup	3 cups cooked

Rice, pre-cooked	1 cup	2 cups cooked
Shallots	1 med	1 tbsp minced
Spaghetti (uncooked)	1 lb	7 cups cooked
Sugar, brown	1 lb	2-1/4 cups packed
Sugar, confectioners	1 lb	3-1/2 to 4 cups sifted
Sugar, granulated	1 lb	2-1/2 cups
Tomatoes (4 medium)	1 lb	1-1/2 cups juiced, chopped pulp
Walnuts, in shell	1 lb	1-1/3 cups nutmeats
Walnuts, shelled	1 lb	4 cups nutmeats

Metric Equivalents

Tablespoons and Ounces (U.S. Customary System)	Grams and Liters (Metric System)
1 pinch = less than 1/8 tsp (dry)	0.5 gram
1 dash = 3 drops to 1/4 tsp (liquid)	1.25 grams
1 tsp (liquid)	5.0 milliliters
3 tsp = 1 tablespoon = 1/2 ounce	14.3 grams
2 tbsp = 1 ounce	28.35 grams
4 tbsp = 2 ounces = 1/4 cup	56.7 grams
8 tbsp = 4 ounces = 1/2 cup (1 stick butter)	113.4 grams
8 tbsp (flour) = about 2 ounces	72.0 grams
16 tbsp = 8 ounces = 1 cup = 1/2 pound	226.8 grams
1 cup	0.24 liters
32 tbsp = 16 ounces = 2 cups = 1 pound	453.6 grams or 0.4536 kilogram
64 tbsp = 32 ounces = 4 cups = 2 pounds	907.0 grams or 0.907 kilogram
4 cups = 1 quart	(roughly) 1 liter

Index

Index